A POCKET GUIDE TO . . .

Human Body
Intricate design that glorifies the Creator

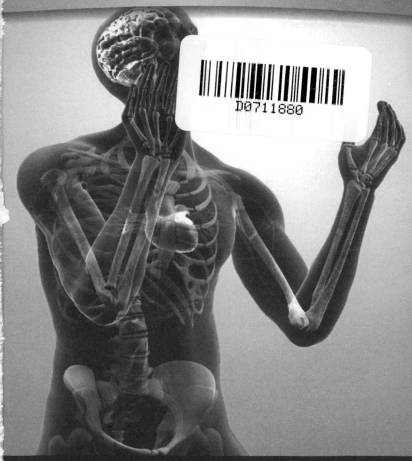

WIRED FOR EXTREMES • BRAIN—SHAPED BY EXPERIENCES • THE SEEING EYE •
THE HEARING EAR • HEART—CONSTANTLY BEATING DEATH • BONES—GOD'S LIVING
GIRDERS • SKIN—OUR LIVING ARMOR • MELANIN—UMBRELLAS OF OUR SKIN •
THE AMAZING HUMAN HAIR • OUR INDEX FINGER—POINTING TO THE CREATOR

A POCKET GUIDE TO . . .

The Human Body

Intricate design that glorifies the Creator

1:1
answersingenesis
Petersburg, Kentucky, USA

ISBN: 1-60092-421-2

Printed in China

www.answersingenesis.org

Table of Contents

Introduction

From the intracacies of the human brain to the functional arrangement of our index finger, the design of the human body proclaims the Creator. While atheists do their best to try and explain how our bodies evolved by random processes, their explanations fall flat when one considers the wonders of our body, and how so many elements fit together "just right" to allow them to function, grow, adapt, repair themselves, and react to the environment. For example:

- Heat from our rapidly beating heart would kill us, if it were not designed with a special lubricated bag that reduces friction.

- Our bones produce new bone throughout adult life, constantly changing shape to handle new stresses, such as extra weight during pregnancy.

- Unlike the wires in a hardwired computer, our brain cells are constantly making new connections and "pruning" old ones that are unused.

- Guarding our bodies is a thin layer of dead cells, arranged into precisely arranged columns that are spot-welded together.

Revel in the creativity of our Creator God as you explore His amazing design of our bodies.

The Human Body— Wired for Extremes

by Heather M. Brinson

You never know what unexpected danger might put your life on the line. But God knows, and He has equipped every human with backup systems that are programmed to respond to all sorts of emergencies.

Astronauts shivering in a broken-down spacecraft far from earth. A woman falling off a cliff. A backpacker encountering a furious bear at a bend in the trail. How could these people possibly survive?

Each depended on incredible biological emergency systems to stay alive.

We live in a cursed world where dangers lurk around every corner. Recognizing the potential threats to our lives, God provided our bodies with contingency plans, ready to activate at a moment's notice. Whatever extra energy or infusion of chemicals our bodies need, whatever quick changes are required for us to make quick decisions or conserve precious resources, the brain is always ready to act.

The beauty of these emergency systems is that we don't have to learn them. Every person begins life with these abilities, which are passed down through the generations, originating in our first parents, Adam and Eve.

Researchers are learning more and more about how our brain switches operations when thrown into hazardous situations. You may never face life-threatening situations, or you may face them only once, but in any case, God has equipped you to have a better chance of surviving. Consider just three examples.

To coldly go

The loud bang was unexpected. At first, the other astronauts thought a crewmember was playing a practical joke. But they soon realized the situation was serious. On April 13, 1970, *Apollo 13* radioed home. "Houston, we've had a problem."

Over the next few days, NASA's Mission Control in Texas and the endangered astronauts banded together to solve nearly each problem thrown at them. They figured out how to preserve batteries and water. The NASA teams even managed to design a makeshift air scrubber to reduce the dangerous levels of carbon dioxide in the small spaceship. But one problem couldn't be solved—the lunar module *Aquarius* was getting cold, almost freezing (around 38°F [3.3°C]).

Initially, the heat given off by the computer systems helped to maintain the temperature in *Aquarius*, but later they were turned off to preserve the precious power. Three days after the explosion, the cold was nearly unbearable. The astronauts never slept. Fred Haise's feet, after getting soaked from a leaky water dispenser, were half frozen. Their food turned into blocks of ice.

How did they manage to survive? Their brains were ready with a contingency plan that NASA could never imagine.

Alone and exposed to near-freezing temperatures, without warm clothes or heaters, and three days away from help. Could you survive? Yes! The brain's hypothalamus (right) is ready for just such emergencies, and it made the difference in the *Apollo 13* mission.

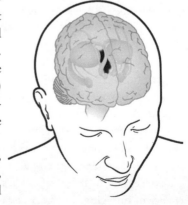

One part of the brain, called the hypothalamus, regulates the body's internal temperature. When we get too hot or too cold, the hypothalamus initiates emergency systems. When the temperature plummeted to a critical low, the astronauts' hypothalamuses responded immediately.

The first defense was to generate heat. Muscles, like computers, produce heat when working. So the astronauts started shivering involuntarily.

The second defense preserved what heat their bodies still contained. As the temperature continued to drop, their brains stimulated the blood vessels just below the skin's surface to constrict, keeping the blood deeper and warmer as it circulated.

Still, it got colder, causing slowed heart rates, and digestion. Their brains initiated the next step. In an effort to protect the vital organs, their brains triggered the blood to concentrate around the heart and brain, keeping those key areas warmer and vital systems functioning. Fingers, toes, and other extremities were left to the cold.

As the astronauts' bodies continued to cool, the nervous systems slowed, and clear thinking was hampered. The astronauts even struggled to understand and remember what Mission Control told them. Their brains were conserving all resources in an effort to survive, and logical thinking was unnecessary for immediate survival.

Finally, the end was in sight. After days of fighting the cold and fear, the astronauts buckled in, ready to restart the engine of the Command Module. Amidst cheers and more than a few tears, they entered earth's atmosphere. The *Apollo 13* mission is commonly known as NASA's successful failure. The astronauts made it home, thanks, in great part, to the incredible design of their bodies.

Pain, pain go away

Hiking alone through the Sierra Nevada Mountains in California had always been one of Amy Racina's favorite pastimes. The beauty of the trees, the silence of the hills, and the warm August air filled Amy with peace and joy. Then the unthinkable happened.

Near the edge of a cliff, the ground suddenly crumbled underneath her feet. She tumbled into space with nothing to catch her but a granite slab 60 feet (18 m) below.

When Amy woke up, she waited for pain to overwhelm her. It didn't. So she sat up and assessed her situation. Her hip was broken in two places, her right kneecap had shattered, and she noticed several other minor fractures, sprains, and dislocations.

Amy knew she was badly hurt, so why wasn't she overwhelmed with pain?

Isolated in remote mountains, her body broken and bleeding after a sixty-foot fall, how could Amy Racina hope to survive? Her brain's periaqueductal gray (right) went right to work, recognizing the threat and initiating an extraordinary survival strategy.

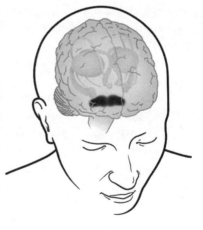

In extreme emergencies, our brain can block pain. If Amy had felt the full force of the pain from all of her injuries, she would have been unable to bind her wounds and drag herself the mile and a half to the nearest trail. The trail offered the only hope of rescue before she bled to death.

Typically, pain is a good thing. It warns us of injury or sickness. It tells us when to slow down or when we've done too much. Few things send us to the doctor faster than intense pain. If we never felt pain, we would rarely notice when we hurt ourselves.

But in life-threatening situations, it's not always good to feel pain. Soldiers in the midst of battle don't always have time to treat bullet wounds. Long-term survival may demand their full attention on the enemy, so the brain can temporarily block the pain.

But how can our brains block pain? Scientists are still trying to understand the details, but the gate control theory suggests that the paths between pain-transmitting nerves can be blocked by natural pain killers.[1] Normally, nerves at the injured site send signals along a path to a projection neuron (the gate) located in the spine, which then forwards the message to the brain.

However, if the pain must be blocked, a special region in the middle of the brain, called the periaqueductal gray, closes the gate by releasing endorphins, natural pain killers more powerful than morphine. Once the danger has passed, the periaqueductal gray will remove the endorphins, allowing pain through the gate.

Once rescuers arrived to lift Amy by helicopter to a hospital, pain flooded over her. The temporary lull in pain had saved her life. Now it was time for the normal process of rest and healing to begin.

Bear in mind

Hiking in the middle of the remote forest in the USA's Yellowstone National Park, 22-year-old Josh Beattie turned the corner and nearly stumbled over a grizzly bear cub at play, blocking his path. But mom was there, too. Suddenly, his heart raced, his breathing increased, and his muscles tensed.

What was happening to Josh?

His brain was preparing to fight or flee. At the first sign of danger, before the problem is fully processed by the logic center, our brain already kicks into gear. In many cases, like touching a hot stove, if we waited until we consciously understood the dangers, our reaction would come too late.

So how does this fight or flight system work?

When danger nears, the hypothalamus (the same part of our brain that regulates body temperature) "flips a switch." Before we have time to think, our brain speeds ahead of us, ordering the release of appropriate chemicals. Our brain also increases blood flow to the muscles, allowing for quick action. Breathing deepens to elevate oxygen intake. Heart rate and pressure increase to speed oxygen delivery. Many nonvital systems temporarily shut down. Growth, digestion, and the immune system stop functioning so that energy is not wasted on systems not required for immediate survival.

But the brain acts differently if the danger is farther away. According to one study, the distance of the threat relates to the area our brain uses to face it.[2] If the angry mother bear appears far away, the part of our brain used for strategy (called the ventromedial prefrontal cortex) activates. But as she draws closer, the focus switches to the fight or flight part of our brain, known as the periaqueductal gray (the same part that controls feeling pain). Essentially, the brain seeks to implement an escape plan before momma bear gets too close.

Far from any trail, hiker Josh Beattie stumbled on two bears, only 25 yards away. Would he survive? Before he even had time to think, his brain initiated emergency procedures. The hypothalamus (see previous image) ordered more blood to the muscles, increased his heart rate, and deepened breathing. Then the periaqueductal gray (see previous image) prepared him to make the ultimate decision: escape or fight?

Time is up. Which will you choose, fight or escape? The answer comes down to the individual. Whether we run or fight is not always clear-cut, and the decision depends on our emotions and the situation. But no matter the emergency, God designed the human brain with the specialized capabilities to help us survive, be it day-to-day hassles or perilous threats to life.

The end but not the limit

At the same time that mankind explores the deep mysteries of the oceans and the awesome glories of the heavens, where the Creator's genius is clearly seen, we are just as amazed by the intricacies scientists constantly discover in the human brain.

The same God who displays His power in space reminds us about His loving care in our own bodies and minds. From the very beginning, God provided for His children even before such protection was needed. Adam and Eve were well-equipped to survive in a fallen world, and so are we.

1. R. Melzack and P. Wall, "Pain Mechanisms: A New Theory," *Science* 19 (November 1965): 971–978.

2. D. Mobbs et al., "When Fear Is Near: Threat Imminence Elicits Prefrontal-Periaqueductal Gray Shifts in Humans," *Science* 24 (August 2007): 1079–1083.

Heather M. Brinson is currently earning dual degrees in English and chemistry from Clemson University. A previously published author, Heather hopes to use her combined abilities in ministry when she graduates.

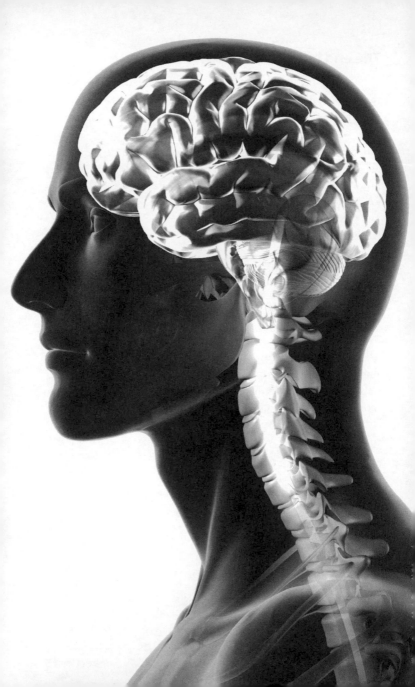

Brain—Shaped By Experiences

by David A. DeWitt

*L*ang Lang was only three. Curious and awkward, he pressed an ivory key for the first time on the big wooden piano—and loved the sound. With practice, the boy born in Shenyang, China, became a prodigy, winning international competitions by age 13. Lang Lang still amazes and inspires audiences, now playing with great symphony orchestras.

If we set our mind to it, we can do really amazing things. The more we practice, the better we become. In addition to music, we can learn to dribble a soccer ball, hit a softball, paint, sing, ride a bike, drive a car, fly a helicopter, or learn any other skill that requires precise muscle control and fine-tuned senses.

Yet acquiring skills would be impossible if our brains were "hardwired" at birth. To sort through all the data that our body's sensors record, the brain has been designed to change. Our brain is not a computer, made of solid-state wires and silicon wafers. It is three pounds of living, growing cells that constantly form new connections and change old ones.

The brain's flexibility enables us to quickly acquire new skills, learn new information, and create new memories. Further, if our brain suffers certain types of injury, brain cells can take over the function of the dead or damaged cells.

Modern imaging tools can now look inside the brain while it is still at work. For the first time, we are beginning to see just how marvelously God designed our brain to adapt to our ever-changing needs.

Music and the brain

Neuroscience researchers have known for years that the brains of musicians have more grey matter in certain areas than most other people. Are they born with these differences, or do their brains change with experience? Neuroscientists have tended toward the latter view but lacked hard evidence.[1]

Recent studies have demonstrated that music training also improves skills in many areas, including fine motor skills and sound discrimination. Some researchers have even noticed improvement in attention, math skills, and geometry tasks.[2] Imaging studies of

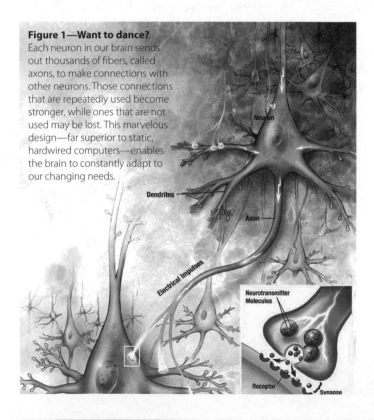

Figure 1—Want to dance?
Each neuron in our brain sends out thousands of fibers, called axons, to make connections with other neurons. Those connections that are repeatedly used become stronger, while ones that are not used may be lost. This marvelous design—far superior to static, hardwired computers—enables the brain to constantly adapt to our changing needs.

Neuron

Dendrites

Axon

Electrical Impulses

Neurotransmitter Molecules

Receptor

Synapse

the brain have confirmed that the networks of neurons associated with these abilities change physically, too.

Scientists have not been able to completely rule out the possibility of predisposition or innate structural differences in the brain that would account for musical ability, but the amount of tissue in different regions of the brain does tend to correlate with the amount of practice and training. Musicians, for example, have more tissue in regions responsible for sound discrimination and finger control. This and other evidence strongly suggests that experience alters the architecture of the brain. Neuroplasticity refers to the changes that take place as the neurons' connections (called synapses) are generated, altered, and reinforced (Figure 1).

Location, location, location

One aspect of the brain that triggered my own interest in neuroscience is how the brain is laid out. The neurons that control our senses and motor skills are arranged into an orderly map in the brain, called a homunculus (Figure 2).

For example, the neurons responsible for touch are laid out in a three-dimensional sequence in the brain, known as a spatial trajectory. If two parts of the body, such as the thumb and index finger, are located next to each other physically, they also have corresponding neurons that are next to each other in the brain. So when scientists attempt to map the sensory neurons in the brain, they find neurons that respond to stimulation of the thumb next to neurons that respond to stimulation of the index finger and so on. The same holds true for neurons that control muscle movement.

Although the neurons in the brain mirror the arrangement of the body parts, they do not mirror the relative size of the body parts. For example, while our arms and legs are much larger than our thumb and lips, they occupy much less space in our brain. The fingers need more space because they require so many more neurons to control fine motor skills and delicate sensations.

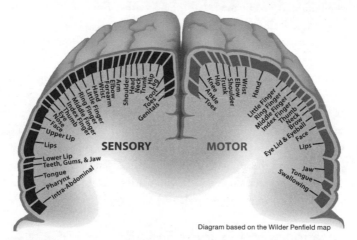

Figure 2—Map of our brain
Our brain functions like a well-organized bookshelf, with different spaces allocated to each sense or motor skill. These books must compete with each other for shelf space. As we increase skills in one area, the brain must take away space from the nearest books.

Our other senses have similar orderly sequences in the brain. For example, the neurons involved in hearing are arranged by pitch, similar to the keys on a piano. Likewise, the neurons responsible for vision are arranged by sectors of our field of view. This creates an interesting challenge because we have two eyes that see overlapping fields of view. To compensate for this, the brain allocates alternating columns of neurons to the left and right eyes.

The overall pattern of neurons in the brain is laid out early in life. In some cases, it is critical that a body part gets the right stimulation at specific times during development. For example, if one eye of a cat is covered during the critical period so that no stimulation occurs, then the cat could be blind in that eye for life. The cat loses its sight because the neurons that would otherwise accept information from that eye are committed to the other eye.

While changes to the brain are possible, they can be limited by prior experience.

Interestingly, if a finger is amputated or the nerve to the finger is destroyed, the neurons that were allocated to that finger become reallocated to the adjacent fingers. For example, if the index finger is lost, the neurons shift to covering the thumb and middle finger. In contrast, if a musician decides to practice with one finger more than all the other fingers, the space allocated for that finger will increase at the expense of the other fingers.

The brain functions like a bookshelf with limited shelf space. If you need to add more pages to one of the books, then the increase needs to come at the expense of pages from other, nearby books on the shelf.

Behaviors or senses that are used more, receive a greater allocation of space in the brain. This explains why individuals who are blind or deaf seem to have heightened sensitivity in other areas.

Practice makes perfect

Neurons make an astonishing number of connections with other neurons. An adult brain has around 100 billion neurons, and just one of those neurons can make tens of thousands of connections.

Initially, neurons send out fibers to a wide target area. Those connections that are repeatedly used become stronger, while those that are unused can be lost in a process called pruning. Neurons are constantly competing with each other for targets. Over time, each neuron becomes responsible for an increasingly smaller area.

Both positive and negative changes can be reinforced. For example, excessive use of alcohol or drugs can lead to changes in neuronal connections. Indeed, drug addiction is likely to be related to changes in neural circuits caused by the drug use.

Since experience alters the brain in both positive and negative ways, it is all the more important to live a godly life. Perhaps this is one reason that the Apostle Paul admonished Christians how to think: "Finally, brothers, whatever is true, whatever is noble, whatever is right, whatever is pure, whatever is lovely, whatever is admirable—if anything is excellent or praiseworthy—think about such things" (Philippians 4:8).

God's design of the brain

The organization and layout of the nerve cells in the human brain is truly remarkable. The brain continues to change and adapt, as well as repair itself, throughout life. The brain follows an overall plan of development but then alters based on experience, stimulation, and the environment. Although I may be biased as a neuroscientist, I believe nothing provides greater testimony than the brain to how we are "fearfully and wonderfully made."

---

1.   C. Gaser and G. Schlaug, "Brain Structures Differ between Musicians and Non-Musicians," *Journal of Neuroscience* 23(27): 9240–9245.

2.   B. Mauk, "Music Training Changes Brain Networks," http://www.dana.org/news/brainin-thenews/detail.aspx?id=21764.

Dr. David A. DeWitt holds a PhD in neuroscience from Case Western Reserve University. Currently a professor of biology and director of the Center for Creation Studies at Liberty University, his primary research efforts have focused on understanding the mechanisms causing cellular damage in Alzheimer's disease.

The Seeing Eye

by David N. Menton

The Bible tells us that God's eternal power and divine nature are clearly seen in the things that He has made. One of the most obvious displays of His creative power is the human eye.

Even Charles Darwin conceded that "to suppose that the eye, with all its inimitable contrivances for adjusting the focus to different distances, for admitting different amounts of light, and for the correction of spherical and chromatic aberration, could have been formed by natural selection, seems, I freely confess, absurd in the highest possible degree."[1]

Nonetheless, having abandoned his Christianity, Darwin was obliged to appeal to the "absurd" to account for the origin of the eye by random change and natural selection.

A living camera

The eye is essentially a living video camera of extraordinary sensitivity. Like any good manmade camera, the eye has a black interior to prevent light scattering, and an automatically focusing lens and adjustable diaphragm to control the light. And like the most sophisticated modern digital cameras, the eye has a light-sensitive layer (the retina) that can adjust to a wide range of brightness.

But unlike any camera made by man, the retina can automatically change its sensitivity to brightness over a range of ten billion to one! The retina's light-sensitive cells (photoreceptors) can perceive a range of light, from bright sunlit snow to a single photon (the smallest unit of light). The eye also has the amazing ability to assemble and repair itself, unlike manmade cameras.

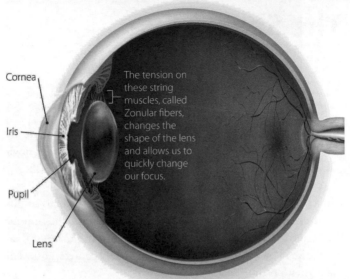

Cornea

Iris

Pupil

Lens

The tension on these string muscles, called Zonular fibers, changes the shape of the lens and allows us to quickly change our focus.

Picture courtesy of JirehDesign.com

Each part of the eye has unique responsibilities to allow us to see. The eye is similar to a camera, yet can do much more. The eye is self-lubricating, self-repairing, and self-cleaning. Unlike any camera, the eye converts images into electrical signals that are sent immediately to the brain, where it processes those signals and makes necessary adjustments.

- **Cornea**
  About four times more powerful than the lens in bringing light into focus, the cornea is the thin covering over the front of the eye.

- **Iris**
  The iris is the colorful part of the eye. It consists of two sets of muscles that work together to open and close the iris diaphragm.

- **Pupil**

  The pupil controls the amount of light let into the eye. The two sets of muscles in the iris control the size of the pupil.

- **Lens**

  The lens is flexible like rubber and can quickly focus by changing its shape.

Looking out a "window"

It is said that a camera is no better than its lens. How good is the lens of the human eye?

Actually, the human eye has two excellent lenses—the cornea and the lens proper. During our development in the womb, embryonic skin over the developing eye turns into a clear window. To be so crystal clear, this special type of skin lacks the blood vessels, hair, and glands in most other skin, though it contains many nerves (and is highly sensitive to touch).

Although we tend to think of the cornea as a protective window rather than a lens, it really functions as a lens. In fact, the cornea is about four times more powerful in bringing light to focus on our retina than the lens itself.

The "rubber" lens

The lens proper, like the cornea, is also derived from embryonic skin and is marvelously transparent. Unlike the fixed cornea, however, the lens can change its focus. This automatic focusing function allows us to quickly focus on any object we look at. Most cameras focus by physically moving their hard lenses, but the lens of the eye is flexible like rubber and can quickly focus by changing its shape.

Since man's fall into sin, much of God's original creation is now less than perfect, and so the lens loses flexibility with age, reducing both its clarity and its ability to focus.

Your brain is showing

While the cornea and lens develop from embryonic skin, most of the eyeball develops in the embryo as a bud from the brain. Think of it, you can actually examine part of someone's brain just by looking them in the eye!

The eyeball buds off the brain in just the right position for it to look out through the lens and cornea. It would be a shame to have eyes in our head, but no windows in the skin to look out through.

The muscular eye

We don't generally think of our eye as a muscular organ, but this small orb has some of the busiest muscles in the body. There are two sets of muscles inside the eye. One set opens and closes the iris diaphragm, admitting different amounts of light. The second set of muscles is attached by "strings" to the perimeter of the lens and changes its shape during focusing.

The muscles of our eyes are some of the busiest muscles in the body. Twelve separate muscles (six on each eye) must move in perfect coordination for us to see the object we are looking at.

The lateral rectus and medial rectus work like reins on a horse to aim the eye left and right. The superior rectus and inferior rectus serve to aim the eye up and down. The superior oblique and inferior oblique serve to rotate the eye like a door knob. The purpose of these oblique muscles is to keep our visual horizon level when we tilt our head from left to right so we don't get dizzy.

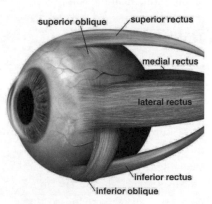

Picture courtesy of JirehDesign.com

There are also three pairs of muscles attached to the outside of the eye. These muscles rotate the eyeball so we can look in different directions without moving our heads. Basically one pair of muscles works like reins on a horse to aim the eye left and right. A second pair of muscles, attached to the top and bottom of the eyeball, aims the eye up and down. Finally, a third set of muscles rotates the eye like a doorknob. The purpose of these last two muscles is to keep our vision level when we tilt the head from side to side, so we don't get dizzy. (The Lord thinks of everything!)

Just think of it. Everywhere we turn our gaze, twelve separate muscles (six on each eye) move in perfect coordination for us to see the object we're looking at. If our eyes are even slightly misaligned, we see double. This remarkable coordination is like a marksman so accurate with a pair of pistols that he can make only one bullet hole every time he fires both guns!

Window wipers and washers

Our eyelids not only protect our eyes and cover them when we sleep or blink, but also serve as window wipers for the cornea. Deep under the upper eyelid, toward the side of the head, each eye has a special reservoir of eye-washing fluid called the lachrymal glands. These glands secrete a watery tear fluid that has just the right acid level (pH) and osmotic (concentration) properties. The fluid also contains special enzymes that keep the eye clean of things that cause infection, and it has special oils to reduce evaporation. It also gives our cornea a smooth surface for optimum vision.

The self-cleaning eye

If you look very closely at your eye, you will notice a small opening on the margin of your upper and lower eyelids near the nose. These holes, called puncta, are attached to pumps that remove the tear fluid as it flows across the eye and drain it into the nose. This continuously flushes our eyes of debris and keeps our cornea from drying out (which can cause blindness).

When we produce too much tear fluid (as in weeping), the layer of liquid over the cornea can get too thick, affecting our vision. As the tear pumps remove the tear fluid and drain it into our nose, we get the sniffles. If too much tear fluid accumulates for our pumps to keep up with it, tears overflow and roll down our cheeks.

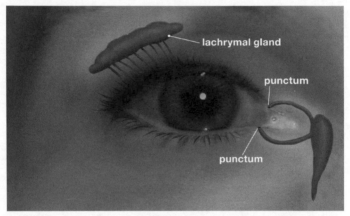

Under the upper eyelid, the lachrymal gland secretes tear fluid for each eye. Tiny holes called puncta drain the tear fluid from the eye and into the nose The amount of tear fluid is optimal for clarity. Have you ever had your eyes well up with tears? If so, you might notice that your vision becomes a little blurry because of the excess tear fluid over your eye. Picture courtesy of John Nyquist

The cornea is not completely smooth. Tear fluid creates a much smoother surface for light to pass through, which enhances clarity. Picture courtesy of John Nyquist

Only Jesus can wipe away our tears

We humans are the only creatures God created that can cry emotional tears. We are also the only object of the redemptive work of Jesus Christ, who came into the world to save us from the wages of sin. What a wonderful comfort that our Heavenly Father has promised to wipe away all our tears of sin, pain, and sadness.

"And God will wipe away every tear from their eyes; there shall be no more death, nor sorrow, nor crying . . . for the former things have passed away" (Revelation 21:4).

---

1. C. R. Darwin, *The Origin of Species by Means of Natural Selection*, 6th ed. (Senate, 1994), pp. 143–144.

* Visit www.answersingenesis.org/media/video/ondemand to watch The Seeing Eye video featuring Dr. Menton.

Dr. David Menton holds his PhD in cell biology from Brown University and is a well-respected author and teacher. He is Professor Emeritus at the Washington University School of Medicine in St. Louis. Dr. Menton has many published works and is one of the most popular speakers for Answers in Genesis–USA.

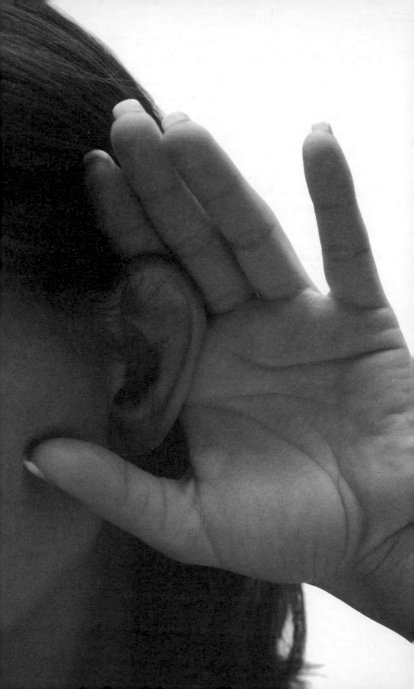

The Hearing Ear

by David N. Menton

*T*he ears can hear everything, from the faint ticking of a small watch to the roar of a jet engine, a range of volume of nearly one million to one! It is fitting that one of the most marvelous organs in the body should be used to hear the Word of God.

Sound

To understand how our ears hear sound we must first understand something about sound itself.

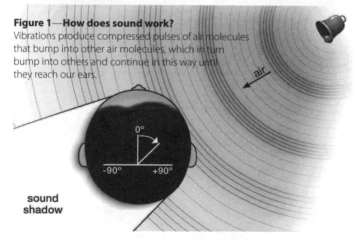

Figure 1—How does sound work?
Vibrations produce compressed pulses of air molecules that bump into other air molecules, which in turn bump into others and continue in this way until they reach our ears.

air

0°

-90° +90°

sound
shadow

Most sounds are produced by something vibrating, such as vocal cords or loudspeakers. These vibrations produce compressed pulses of air molecules that bump into other air molecules, which in turn bump into others and continue in this way until they reach our ears (Figure 1). The ear of a young person can sense as few as 20 pulses per second (for low-pitched sounds) and as many as 20,000 pulses per second (for high-pitched sounds).

The three parts of the ear

Long before the radio was invented, the ear was designed to convert pulses of air into electrical signals. To accomplish this marvel, God gave the ear three parts—the outer ear, the middle ear, and the inner ear (Figure 2). Each part has a different role in locating and converting signals that our brain can use.

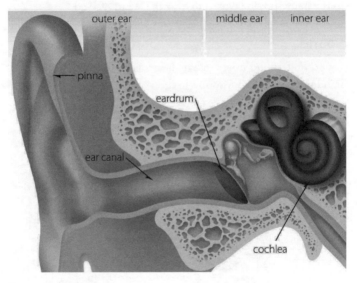

Figure 2—Outer ear
The three parts of the outer ear are the pinna (which is the part of the ear we can see), the ear canal, and the eardrum. Sound waves are caught by the pinna, travel through the ear canal, and cause the eardrum to vibrate.

In a series of complex steps, these three parts are designed to conduct sound through three radically different media—air, bone, and fluid (mostly water).

Outer ear

The outer ear includes the pinna, the ear canal, and the eardrum.

The part of the ear that we see, called the pinna, is commonly known simply as the "ear." It has a complicated cup-like shape designed to catch the sound waves from the air. Having two ears helps us to detect what direction sounds come from. Not only can they detect sounds from the left or right, but our pinnae can detect sounds in front, behind, above, or below us.

The ear canal is about 1 inch (2.5 cm) long and a little over 0.33 inches (0.8 cm) in diameter. It efficiently channels sound waves to the eardrum. Lining the ear canal are special glands that produce earwax (cerumen). This wax lubricates the ear canal, preventing irritation and fighting bacteria.

For most people, the ear canal is self-cleaning. Ear wax traps dust particles, which are then removed from the ear canal (along with the wax) by an amazing conveyor-belt mechanism.

The eardrum (tympanic membrane) plays the final and starring role in the outer ear. Sound waves entering the ear canal cause the eardrum to vibrate. The minute movements of the eardrum are then passed on to the small bones in the middle ear.

Middle ear

The function of the middle ear is to amplify the sound vibrations of the eardrum. The vibrations must be compressed into a much smaller area.

This is accomplished by a sequence of three small bones in the middle ear, known collectively as ossicles (Figure 3). The ossicles are the smallest bones in the body (the smallest bone weighs .0001 ounces (0.3 cg)). They are the only bones that never grow larger from the time of birth.

Vibrations produced in the eardrum are passed to the first bone, called the hammer (malleus), whose "handle" is attached to the eardrum. This bone, in turn, passes its vibrations to a bone called the anvil (incus). Next, the vibration is transmitted to a bone that looks like a stirrup, called the stapes. Finally, the "foot plate," located on the stirrup, is inserted into a small oval window, which opens into the inner ear (Figure 3).

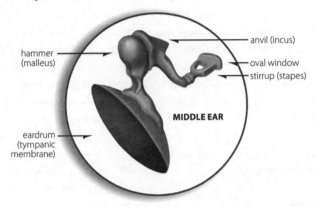

Figure 3—Middle ear
The function of the middle ear is to amplify the sound vibrations of the eardrum. Vibrations from the eardrum are passed to the hammer, then the anvil, and finally the stirrup. Because the vibrations of the eardrum are compressed into the much smaller area of the stirrup foot plate, there is a 20-fold increase in pressure.

Amplification results because the surface area of the eardrum is much greater than the foot plate of the stirrup, thus concentrating the energy over a smaller area and resulting in over a 20-fold increase in pressure. The foot plate moves in and out, like a piston, producing waves in the fluid of the inner ear.

Inner ear

The bony chamber of the inner ear is shaped like a small snail shell, from which it gets its Latin name cochlea (Figure 4). The function of the cochlea is to take the mechanical vibrations from the ossicles (and ultimately the eardrum) and convert them into electrical signals understandable to the brain.

Figure 4—Inner ear

The cochlea, the organ in the inner ear, contains three canals that spiral around inside (Figure 4). The middle canal, called the cochlear duct, contains the organ of Corti (Figure 5). This organ converts mechanical energy produced by the eardrum into electrical energy.

middle canal (cochlear duct)

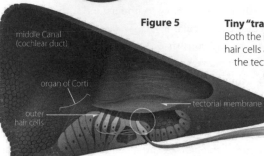

Figure 5

middle Canal (cochlear duct)

organ of Corti

outer hair cells

tectorial membrane

Tiny "trapdoors"

Both the inner and outer hair cells are attached to the tectorial membrane (Figures 5 and 6). When sound waves cause the organ of Corti to bounce up and down, the tectorial membrane wiggles the attached hairs. The wiggling of these hairs causes small "trapdoors" on the tips of the hairs to open and close (Figure 7), permitting electrically charged particles (ions) to enter the hairs. This movement of ions generates electrical signals that are sent to the brain, where they are processed and interpreted.

Figure 7

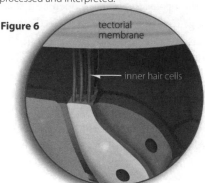

Figure 6

tectorial membrane

inner hair cells

Inside the cochlea are three canals. The middle canal is a spiral, filled with a special fluid. Running within this spiral canal is yet another fluid-filled channel called the cochlear duct (Figures 4 and 5). As the piston movement of the middle ear causes waves to travel through the fluid in the cochlea, the cochlear duct bounces up and down.

The organ of Corti

Inside the cochlear duct is a strip of tissue known as the organ of Corti, one of the most remarkable organs in the body. It is very complex but worth the effort to try to understand it. Here the ear converts signals at the molecular level.

This organ essentially consists of three rows of outer hair cells and one row of inner hair cells (Figure 6). The tops of the cells have tiny "hairs" (thus the name "hair cells"). These hairs are actually cilia that are much smaller than a hair on our bodies. In fact, they are too small to be seen individually, even with a light microscope.

The tips of some of the hairs are attached to an overlying spiral membrane called the tectorial membrane (Figure 6). When the organ of Corti bounces up and down, the tectorial membrane wiggles the hairs.

The wiggling of the hairs causes small molecular "trapdoors" on the tips of the hairs to open and close, permitting electrically charged particles (ions) to enter the hairs (Figure 7). Incredibly, the molecular trapdoors are controlled by molecular springs that attach to adjustable molecular brackets.

It staggers the mind to think of tiny molecular trapdoors opening and closing at a rate between 20 and 20,000 times per second, admitting charged ions into the tips of the hairs. This movement of ions generates electrical signals that are sent to the brain, where they are processed and interpreted.

God made the hearing ear

The Bible declares, "The hearing ear and the seeing eye, the Lord has made them both" (Proverbs 20:12, NKJV). It logically follows that God, who made the hearing ear, is Himself able to hear. The Psalmist asks, "He that planted the ear, shall he not hear? He that formed the eye, shall he not see?" (Psalms 94:9, KJV).

Indeed, the Creator is not limited by physical ears and eyes. He can hear our very thoughts and see into our hearts. This is a frightening thing for the unbelieving sinner, who would not want a perfect God listening in on his every word and thought. But for the believing Christian whose sins have been covered by the blood of Christ, a hearing (and seeing) God is a profound blessing and comfort.

---

* Visit www.answersingenesis.org/media/video/ondemand to watch The Hearing Ear video featuring Dr. Menton.

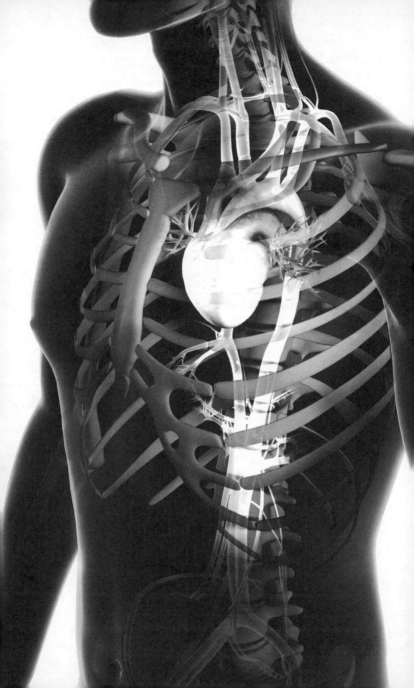

Heart—Constantly Beating Death

by Heather M. Brinson

Our lives hang on a thread. A constant flow of rich blood must reach cells throughout the body, delivering oxygen and essential nutrients to our extremities, while removing waste products like carbon dioxide. Stop the flow for just a few minutes, and life will cease.

How did the Creator ensure a steady flow? He gave us a pump made of soft flesh, not of hard steel. Estimates vary, but this powerful muscle pushes blood through at least 1,500 miles (2,500 km) of blood vessels, some as narrow as one red blood cell. The heart must keep beating 100,000 times a day without tiring or malfunctioning.

We are a walking miracle, exquisitely designed for life on earth. Just consider three engineering challenges that our heart has to overcome.

Challenge #1: Running in two directions at once

Blood needs to flow through two separate circuits of blood vessels at the same time. The first circuit gathers the blood from the body and sends it to the lungs so it can pick up oxygen and get rid of carbon dioxide. The second circuit picks up the oxygen-rich blood returned from the lungs and sends it to the rest of the body. But we are given only one heart to pump blood in these two directions. How can this challenge be overcome?

Solution: Two pumps in one

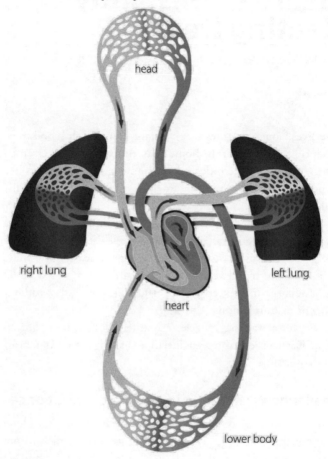

Figure 1—Two pumps in one
The right side of the heart pumps blood through the lungs, while the left side pumps blood through the tissues of the head and body.

The heart is actually two pumps in one. In the mother's womb, the baby's heart starts out as a simple, large tube. As the baby grows, however, the Creator designed the tube so that it loops back, forming a kink. The sides fuse together, forming a wall between two separate compartments. As the rest of the heart forms, the two sides remain separate, essentially becoming two separate pumps.

Each of these pumps has its own two-chamber pumping system (Figure 1). The muscles in one chamber contract and squeeze out blood, while muscles in the other chamber relax and fill with blood. The heart continually wrings out blood by a twisting motion, like wringing a mop. Wringing out liquid is more efficient than the direct squeezing of typical man-made pumps.

The same action squeezes blood out of both pumps—filling one chamber while it empties the other chamber. But this presents a problem. The left side must create six times more force than the right side to move the blood throughout the body.[1] (More force is necessary because it's harder to move blood to the rest of the body than through the nearby lungs.) To compensate, the left side has been designed with more powerful muscles.

Challenge #2: Running in place

The human body has an amazing ability to keep organs stable as we run, jump, and twirl. That might seem easy for kidneys or our bladder, but the heart presents an extra difficulty. It is pumping vigorously all the time. How can it keep moving without sliding around inside the ribcage or overheating?

Solution: A two-layered sac

To protect this nonstop muscle, God placed it in a special two-layered bag, called the pericardial sac. The tough outer layer of the sac, called the fibrous pericardium, anchors to the diaphragm, while the inner layer, called the serous pericardium, attaches tightly to the heart. A special lubricant fluid between the two layers allows the heart to slide around with little friction. If it were not for this marvelous lubricated sac, the beating heart would create enough heat to kill us.

The pericardial sac is just one more amazing feature that naturalistic evolution has a hard time explaining, but it makes sense within a biblical worldview.

Challenge #3: Running continuously

The nerves responsible for our senses tire quickly. Have you ever smelled a strong odor and then stopped noticing the smell? Your nose's nerve cells simply stopped firing. You literally stopped smelling. The nerves to the heart, in contrast, can never stop firing for as long as we live. Ever.

Solution: A pacemaker

How can this difficulty be resolved? God designed a separate system of nerves called the autonomic nervous system. These nerves differ from the nerves of our five senses because they continuously transmit without fail. They don't get overwhelmed with information (like the strain on your eyes from staring too long at a bright tie-dyed shirt), so they don't tire out.

Yet our hearts are different from typical autonomic systems. Most systems, like digestion, don't have to run constantly. The heart, on the other hand, must function all the time. So God gave the heart a built-in pacemaker that allows it to run regularly, without active outside control.

Sitting on the upper right side of the heart is a cluster of specialized cells called the sinoatrial node. They generate electrical impulses that stimulate the muscles in the upper chambers to contract. The signal continues moving down to another cluster of cells above the lower chambers, which then fire.

These electrical impulses ebb and flow in regular waves, without the need for direct input from the brain.

If needed, however, the brain can directly control heart rate and blood pressure. The brain constantly monitors the heart to evaluate when to step in.

During a rigorous tennis game, for example, our muscles need more oxygen to burn. So the brain signals the heart directly to increase the heart rate. At the same time, the heart stimulates the adrenal glands to release the chemical adrenaline. Adrenaline then keeps the heart rate up without further assistance from the brain.

When the tennis match ends and the muscles relax, the brain signals the adrenal glands to stop producing adrenaline, and the heart rate returns to normal.

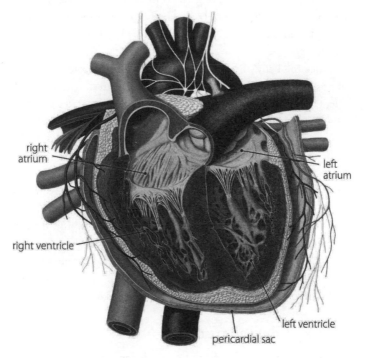

Figure 2—Anatomy of the heart
The heart consists of two separate pumps that pump blood through two separate chambers—an atrium and a ventricle. While one chamber fills up, the other one is squeezed out. Surrounding the heart is a protective layer known as the pericardial sac. © Dorling Kindersley

A healthy hole

Ever wondered what a baby does with his lungs before he's born? He can't breathe air inside the womb. His lungs are not used. Instead, his blood vessels are temporarily attached to his mother's placenta, where they absorb nutrients and oxygen.

The lung develops until birth, without being called upon to function. In fact, a baby can be born without lungs and survive until the placenta is removed. In contrast, the heart is critical to life from the start. It's the only vital organ that must function from the beginning stage of its development (the heart starts beating at five weeks).

Since the baby's heart does not yet need to devote one of its pumps to circulating blood to the lungs, the heart develops a small hole, called the foramen ovale, in the wall that separates the two pumps. The baby also develops a small vein, called the ductus arteriosus, which allows blood to bypass the lungs and move directly to the body.

At birth, a marvelous transformation takes place. When the lungs inflate and the baby takes his first breath, the pressure in the heart shifts, forcing a flap over the foramen ovale to close the hole. The body also produces chemicals that cause the bypass artery to close.

By marvelous design, the baby emerges from its watery home and breathes the air without a glitch. Blood begins pumping to the lungs to absorb oxygen without a moment's delay.

Running from the truth

Despite the marvels of the heart's design, something is terribly wrong. No matter how hard we try to avoid it, our heart will eventually fail. Without Christ, we are like the walking dead, just biding our time until the inevitable end.

Every heartbeat should remind us about the shortness of life. Sin has corrupted every man's heart, and we can't do anything to stop it. We need a new heart, both literally and spiritually.

Fortunately, the same God who designed our hearts to sustain physical life also designed a miraculous way for us to obtain a new spiritual "heart" that will beat for eternity. He sent His Son, Jesus Christ, down to this planet to become a man and shed His blood in payment for our sin. Through His sacrifice, Jesus offers the gift of eternal life to all who will trust in Him.

> "I [God] will give you a new heart and put a new spirit within you; I will take the heart of stone out of your flesh and give you a heart of flesh" (Ezekiel 36:26).

---

1.   http://www.acbrown.com/lung/Lectures/RsCrcl/RsCrclFlow.htm.

Bones—God's Living Girders

by David N. Menton

Bones may not look very lively, but our life depends on a boney skeleton that is an engineering marvel. Bones are often associated with death, like the dry bones of Ezekiel 37:1–14, but our bones are very much alive with cells, blood vessels, nerves, and pain receptors. Indeed, bones are capable of growing, repairing, and even changing their shape to meet the demands we place on them.

Lots of bones

The adult human skeleton consists of about 206 bones. However, the number varies with age. At birth the human body has about 300 bones, but as the body ages and matures, many of these bones fuse together. The adult skull (without its lower jaw), for example, appears to be one bone, but in fact is made up of 22 fused bones: 8 in the skull proper and 14 in the face. The clavicle (collar bone) is the last bone to completely fuse, about the age of 25.

Two types of bone

The mature skeleton has two basic types of bone, compact bone and spongy bone. One offers brute strength, while the other has a sophisticated design that provides strength with the least possible weight.

Compact bone

The strong tubular shaft of long bones, such as our thigh bone (femur), is made of compact bone. Compact bone itself appears to be completely solid but is actually permeated with many blood vessels running lengthwise within hollow tunnels, called Volkmann's canals. Surrounding each of these canals are con-

compact bone

spongy bone

centric rings, or layers, of bone that form osteons. This architecture helps give compact bone its great strength.

Spongy bone

Spongy bone occurs mostly inside each end of long bones. Spongy bone receives its name from its appearance, not because it can be squeezed like a sponge.

The surface area of spongy bone is vastly greater than that of compact bone, so it is mostly in this type of bone that calcium and phosphorus are stored and removed to maintain mineral balance in our body fluids. Each of the little beams of spongy bone is oriented precisely to impart the greatest strength for the load placed on the bone. Amazingly, when the load placed on bone changes, such as during pregnancy, the spongy bone can change its shape to best accommodate the new load.

A bone's function

Bones serve three kinds of critically important functions in our body—mechanical functions, maintenance of mineral levels, and blood production.

Mechanical functions—protection, support, and movement

First, bones have several mechanical functions. For example, they protect the body's vital organs; they serve as a framework to which the muscles and organs are attached; and they allow the body to move by means of muscles contracting across joints.

Maintenance of mineral levels

A second important function for bone is to help maintain precise levels of calcium and phosphorus in our blood and tissue fluids (a process called mineral homeostasis). Bone serves as a depot for storing and removing these minerals as needed. Among other things, calcium is vital for cells to stick together and for muscles to contract, while phosphorus is an essential ingredient in many complex chemicals, such as DNA and RNA.

Blood production in bone marrow

Finally, an exceedingly important function of bone is to produce blood in bone marrow. The marrow produces both red and white blood cells. Red blood cells are essential for carrying oxygen to all the cells of our body, while white blood cells fight disease and infections.

Special cells in the marrow, called megakaryocytes, produce something else for blood, called platelets. These cell fragments circulate in the blood and are important for blood clotting that patches holes in blood vessels.

A bone's strength

The long bones of our body, such as in our limbs, need special designs for strength.

Rather than solid rods, which bend easily, our longer bones are essentially tubes. Engineers have found that, pound for pound, tubes are stronger and resist bending better than solid rods.

Bone itself is a remarkably strong material. It is as strong as cast iron and resists bending as well as steel, though bone is only one-third of steel's weight.

Much of the strength of bone stems from the fact that bone is what engineers refer to as a composite material. Composite materials are made up of two components, a matrix and reinforcement, that work together to produce enhanced strength. An ancient example is brick made of clay and straw. Modern examples include reinforced concrete and fiberglass.

Bone has the right mix of two very different components: a very hard inorganic material called hydroxylapatite and a tough, fibrous organic material called collagen (the protein of leather). The crystal material makes up about 70% of the dry weight of bone, while collagen makes up most of the remaining 30%.

If bones were made up entirely of hydroxylapatite, they would shatter under a load. If they were made entirely of collagen, they would be rubbery. Instead, they have a perfect balance of both.

Bone's development

Cartilage in the womb

Most bones in our body began as cartilage while we were still in the womb. (Cartilage is a rubbery-like material that gives the flexibility to our nose and ears.) The advantage of cartilage over bone in the early stages of growth is that cartilage can grow from within (interstitial growth) as well as at its surface (appositional growth). Bone, on the other hand, can only grow by adding to its surface, much like the way we make a snowball grow to make a snowman.

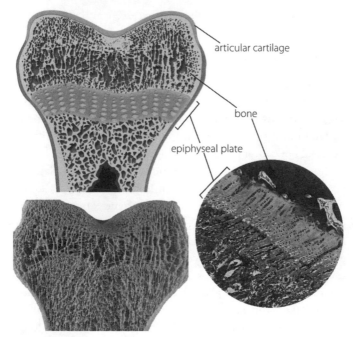

Figure 1—Bone development

WHILE BONES GROW, they still need to stay strong and functional, especially at the joints. So new bone can't grow at the surface, where a permanent layer of smooth cartilage (called *articular cartilage*) allows the joints to function. So God designed special *epiphyseal plates* below the surface. These plates, which are made out of cartilage (the rubbery material in our noses and ears), can grow from within and be replaced with bone.

WHEN BONES STOP GROWING, the cartilage of the growth plates is completely replaced by bone. Once the cartilage is gone, further growth is impossible. So it is easy to tell if a bone came from an adult or a child.

During growth, cartilage is gradually replaced with bone by a process called endochondral ossification. First, calcium infiltrates the cartilage with calcium salts, forming a very brittle calcified cartilage. Then this temporary form of cartilage serves as a framework on which bone will form, much like applying plaster to chicken wire. In time, bone replaces the cartilage except at the ends, where cartilage is retained to form joints.

Growing in length

It is easy to understand how a bone can grow in thickness by adding to its surface, but it is less obvious how a bone grows in length. The ends are capped with a special articular cartilage necessary to form the joints, and the joint would be destroyed if bone were laid down over articular cartilage.

So special cartilage growth plates, called epiphyseal plates, are necessary for long bones to grow in length. These plates, located near each end, bridge the bones' width (Figure 1). Because these growth plates are made of cartilage, they can grow from within. This permits the bone to lengthen without disturbing the cartilage on the ends. As the plates grow in thickness, bone progressively replaces the cartilage (by endochondral ossification, described above).

The growth of these plates is controlled by a growth hormone made in the pituitary gland. When we reach our full height, the growth plates are completely replaced by bone and are no longer responsive to growth hormone.

As long as the growth plates persist and growth hormone is available, an individual can theoretically get taller and taller. The tallest human in modern history was Robert Pershing Wadlow of Alton, Illinois, who at the time of his death in 1940 was 8 feet 11 inches tall! This man, known as the Alton Giant, would have been almost as tall as Goliath of Gath who measured a little over 9 feet tall (1 Samuel 17:4).

Bone makers and bone breakers

Bones stop growing in length when we reach adulthood. But for the rest of our lives bones must continue to be maintained and change shape, repairing damage and responding to changing demands, such as shifting weight during pregnancy. So God designed a mechanism that allows bone to be both formed and removed where necessary (Figure 2).

The cells that make bone are called osteoblasts (which means "bone maker"), and those that remove bone are called osteoclasts (which means "bone breaker").

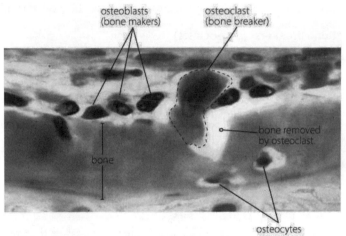

Figure 2—Bone makers and bone breakers
Bones are not dead, solid rods. They're very much alive, filled with two kinds of cells—"bone makers" (osteoblasts) and "bone breakers" (osteoclasts). These cells are constantly at work, repairing and reshaping the bone. As osteoblasts make new bone, however, they eventually get buried in their own bone material and are called osteocytes.

"Bone makers" (osteoblasts)

Osteoblasts don't make the crystal part of bone (hydroxylapatite) directly. They first secrete bone matrix, which initially consists entirely of organic material, including the fibrous protein collagen. Bone matrix attracts minerals, such as calcium and phosphorus, which are in our body fluids. Over time, the minerals accumulate to form the crystal hydroxylapatite.

As osteoblasts make bone matrix, many become trapped in the matrix, "buried alive" like flies stuck in amber. These buried cells are called osteocytes. To remain alive, these cells must maintain contact with one another. They do so by means of dozens of little projections (technically called "processes") that give them a spidery-like appearance. Starting with the closest blood vessel, nutrients and gases are carried from cell to cell by means of these processes, which pass through microscopic canals called canaliculi.

"Bone breakers" (osteoclasts)

Osteoclasts are relatively large cells with many nuclei that remove both the mineral and organic components of bone. They secrete an acid that dissolves the mineral of bone, and enzymes that break down the organic components of bone, including collagen.

During the growth phase of our life, osteoblasts make bone faster than the osteoclasts remove it. When growth is completed, God designed the osteoblasts and osteoclasts to work in harmony, constantly replacing bone without growth. It is believed that this constant replacement of our skeletal tissue serves to repair microfractures that occur in our bones.

As we get older, osteoclasts may remove bone faster than osteoblasts make it, resulting in a reduction of bone density known as osteoporosis. For unknown reasons, osteoporosis affects women more than men. One thing we do know is that bone density increases in response to load from weight or exercise, but prolonged confinement to bed (or weightlessness, such as experienced by astronauts) can result in loss of bone density. So exercise makes good sense to potentially reduce the effects of osteoporosis without drugs.

Jesus's bones were pulled out of joint for our sins

When we sin, it affects us right down to our bones. As the psalmist lamented: "Have mercy on me, O Lord, for I am weak; O Lord, heal me, for my bones are troubled" (Psalm 6:2).

The psalmist gave some remarkable prophesies about what Jesus would have to suffer on the cross to pay for our sins—a suffering that went to His very bones (Psalm 22:17). His bones would not be broken (Psalm 34:20), but—even more agonizing—all his bones would be pulled out of joint (Psalm 22:14).

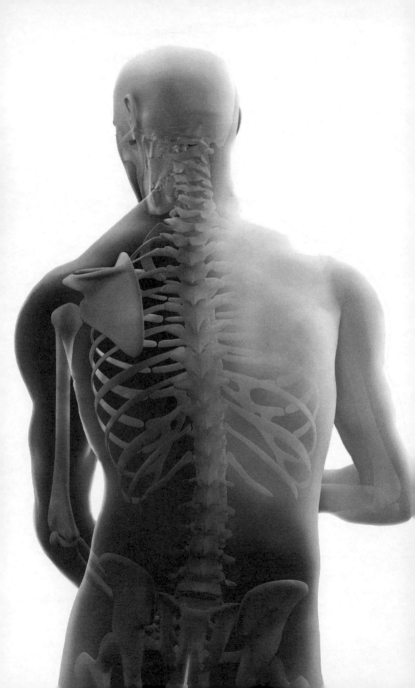

Skin—Our Living Armor

by David N. Menton

You have perhaps heard that "beauty is more than skin deep." While that is certainly true, the skin itself is beautiful and tells us a lot about people. For example, we recognize one another mostly by the skin on our face.

The skin's blood supply and facial muscles even permit us to tell on sight when people are happy, sad, angry, or embarrassed. The skin is the largest organ in our body (weighing about 10 pounds [4.5 kg] in the adult) and covers the entire surface of our body, including our eyes, where the skin covering is conveniently transparent. Being on the surface, skin is the most accessible organ of our body, and thus must be marvelously resistant to our vain efforts to "improve" it with pigments, chemicals, punctures, and tattoos.

Skin—thick and thin

Skin is generally classified as thick skin (on our palms and soles) and thin skin (on the rest of our body). With callouses, thick skin can reach thicknesses of nearly half an inch (13 mm). Thin skin varies in thickness from about 0.5 mm on the eyelid to about 2 mm on the back (1 mm is about the thickness of a dime). Skin is made up of three major layers called the epidermis, dermis, and hypodermis. Each of these layers serves its own vitally important functions.

Figure 1—Three layers of our skin
Our body armor consists of three separate but connected layers. Each performs very different functions, but all are essential to our health and survival. Image © Dorling Kindersley

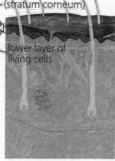

thin layer of dead cells (stratum corneum)

lower layer of living cells

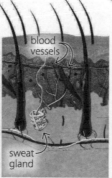

blood vessels

sweat gland

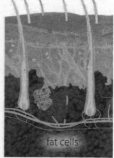

fat cells

Epidermis—The body's "miracle wrap"
On the surface of our bodies is a thin layer of dead cells less than the thickness of shrink wrap. These tightly welded cells serve as an extremely effective first line of defense against the outside world. Below this layer are specialized cells that continually replenish the lining of dead cells.

Dermis—The body's leather
The second layer of our body armor is the dermis, made of tough collagen fibers. These fibers are woven together like fabric to keep our skin strong and flexible. This layer also houses a network of small blood vessels and sweat glands that keep our body temperature constant despite the changing extremes of the outside world.

Hypodermis—Backup and support
The third layer of our body armor provides backup and support. Here body fat is stored for energy, sweat glands produce sweat, and hair grows.

Epidermis—The skin's outermost layer

The body's "miracle wrap"

The outer layer of our skin, the epidermis, is subdivided into two layers: a thin surface layer of dead cells, called the stratum corneum, and a deeper layer of living cells. The stratum corneum is made up of tightly connected dead cells called corneocytes that form a barrier between the living cells of our body and the outside world.

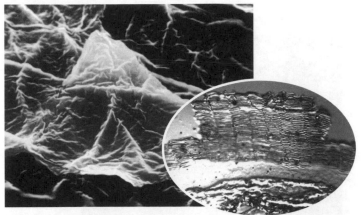

Figures 2 and 3: Thin skin
Most of our body is covered with a type of skin called "thin skin." It is made of special cells (above) that are designed to die and lock together into precisely arranged columns (bottom). Each cell is tightly attached to its neighbor by over one hundred little "spot welds," called desmosomes, which give the skin amazing strength.

If we suddenly lost our stratum corneum, death would quickly follow from massive fluid loss and bacterial invasion. Amazingly, over most of the surface of our body, this critically important dead layer measures less than half the thickness of refrigerator shrink wrap. Indeed, we might call the stratum corneum "miracle wrap."

In thin skin, the dead cells are flattened like thin pancakes and are stacked on top of one another in precise columns (Figures 2 and 3). Each cell is tightly attached to its neighbors on top and bottom by over a hundred little "spot welds" called desmosomes. This tight bond is necessary for the dead layer to resist wear and tear.

In the thick skin on our palms and soles, the epidermis, and particularly the stratum corneum, is much thicker than thin skin. Here the corneocytes themselves are thicker and interlock like jigsaw puzzle pieces (Figure 4). Thick skin is designed to provide high resistance to wear and shearing on the much-used surfaces of our palms and soles.

Cell turnover in the epidermis

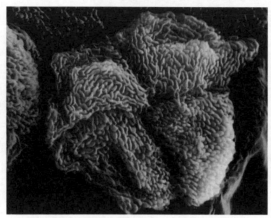

Figure 4: Thick skin
The palms of our hands and soles of our feet experience much more wear and tear than thin skin. So they have a special type of skin called "thick skin," made of much thicker cells that lock together like a jigsaw puzzle.

The main function of the living layer of the epidermis is to produce the dead cells of the stratum corneum. As they mature, these cells become filled with strong protein fibers called keratins. It takes about 28 days for the new cells produced in the lowest level of the living epidermis to rise up to the surface of the skin.

Every minute we lose about 30 to 40 thousand dead skin cells from the surface of our skin, which equals about 9 pounds of dead cells every year!

If the epidermis just kept adding new cells, our skin would grow thicker and thicker. To prevent this, the dead cells on the outer surface must regularly loosen their tight bonds and fall off the surface of the skin in a precisely controlled manner. In fact, every minute we lose about 30,000 to 40,000 dead corneocytes from the surface of our skin. That comes to about 9 pounds (4 kg) of dead cells every year! We are not aware of the loss because normally these cells fall off individually.

The outer cells can't fall off too quickly, however. If cell loss exceeded cell production by only a few percent, we would quickly lose our stratum corneum and die. Amazingly, cell loss precisely matches cell production.

Dermis—The second layer of skin

The body's "leather"

The dermis, which lies just below the epidermis, is comprised of very strong fibers made of a protein called collagen. The collagen fibers are exquisitely woven into a very complex tissue that in animals, such as cows, serves as our source of leather. The dermis accounts for most of the skin's strength and is highly resistant to tearing. While the dermis must be strong, it must also be elastic and flexible to permit us to move comfortably. Though the collagen fibers themselves are very inelastic, the way they are woven permits the skin to stretch much like a double-knit fabric. Special elastic fibers woven through the dermis help restore stretched skin back to its relaxed condition, much like the rubber strands in the elastic waistband of underwear.

Figure 5: Heat regulation
The second layer of skin, the dermis, is filled with a complex network of blood vessels and valves. They allow the body to divert blood near the skin to release heat and cool the body. The many loops increase the surface area, like an efficient radiator.

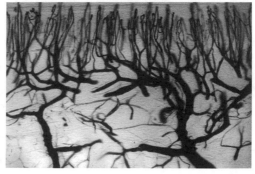

The body's "radiator"

Another important function of the dermis is regulating our body's temperature. When our body gets too warm, heat in our blood needs to reach the surface of the skin so that it can dissipate into the air. To control how much heat reaches the surface, blood vessels in the dermis have valves that can divert the blood into smaller vessels (capillaries) in different levels of the dermis (Figure 5). Under control of the brain, blood is diverted to fill these capillaries and dissipate heat. The regulation of heat is further aided by sweat glands that pass through both the dermis and epidermis. We have about three million sweat glands in our skin that can secrete up to about three quarts of sweat per hour. Sweat, which is largely water, evaporates off the surface of our skin, giving a cooling effect.

Hypodermis—The skin's deepest layer

The hypodermis, the skin's deepest layer, can vary immensely in thickness. Most of this layer is body fat that serves as the principal source of energy when we are deprived of food. Strands of collagen pass through the fat of the hypodermis, anchoring the skin to underlying muscle and bone, limiting the mobility of our skin.

Most of the length of our hair follicles and sweat glands resides in the hypodermis. Indeed, it is here that hair grows and the sweat glands produce their sweat. When we lose skin in a deep abrasion, the surviving sweat ducts and hair follicles serve as a source of new skin. Without these numerous sources of new skin cells, we would require a skin transplant for even a skinned knee.

Conclusion

God's handiwork in creation is evident in everything He has made—even our skin. Like so many other things, we take the protective functions of skin for granted. But let us thank God for our skin, which is so essential for our very lives. Most of all, let us thank our Lord and Savior who endured those who pressed a crown of thorns through the skin of His brow and lashed the skin of His back to shreds. By His stripes we are healed from sin, death, and hell (1 Peter 2:24).

"For I know that my Redeemer lives, and He shall stand at last on the earth; and after my skin is destroyed, this I know, that in my flesh I shall see God, whom I shall see for myself, and my eyes shall behold, and not another. How my heart yearns within me!" (Job 19:25–27).

Melanin—Umbrellas of Our Skin

by David N. Menton

Umbrellas are not just for rain; they can also shade us from the sun. As Jonah sat sulking over God's mercy toward Nineveh, God prepared a large plant—like a big umbrella—to shade him from the beating sun (Jonah 4:6). Just as our merciful God protected Jonah, He has provided our skin with millions of tiny umbrellas to protect us from the sun's damaging rays.

Dangerous ultraviolet rays

In addition to visible light, the sun produces invisible light called ultraviolet (UV), which has a greater effect on our skin. Depending on the amount of exposure, UV light can be either beneficial or damaging. With moderate exposure, UV promotes the production of vitamin D in our skin, an essential for building strong bones and teeth. In larger doses, however (and especially at a certain wavelength), UV light can damage our skin, producing burns, premature skin aging, wrinkling, mutations, and skin cancer.

Melanin to the rescue

Like all good sunshades, the umbrellas in our skin are darkly colored. The dark pigment in our skin, called melanin, is typically black or brown. This protein is produced by special cells, called melanocytes, which are located in the lowest level of our epidermis (the surface layer of our skin, Figure 1).

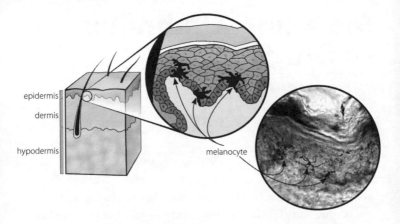

Figure 1—Manufacturing melanin
Melanin is the pigment primarily responsible for our skin color. Melanin is produced in special cells, called melanocytes, located in the lower layer of our epidermis (the surface layer of our skin).

Melanocytes themselves are not the umbrellas of our skin. They merely produce the melanin for our skin, in the form of tiny granules called melanosomes.

Then they transfer the granules to certain epidermal cells in the lowest layer of our epidermis, where they block the damaging UV that penetrates our skin. In other words, melanocytes are like pigment factories that ship pigments (melanosomes) to other cells where the pigment is needed.

The mechanism to transfer the granules is itself amazing. The melanocyte is a highly branched cell with long, slender projections, or processes (Figure 2). The melanocyte makes the melanosomes which then move out to the tips of the cell processes. The epidermal cells then "bite off" the tips of these processes, bringing the granules inside their cell.

Once inside, the melanosomes are moved and arranged to form a dark "cap" over the epidermal cell's nucleus. This pigmented cap serves as a tiny umbrella for the nucleus, specifically blocking the most damaging wavelength of the UV light (Figure 2).

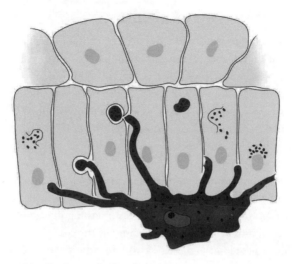

Figure 2—Distributing melanin

Once melanin is manufactured, it is packaged into tiny granules, called melanosomes, ready for shipment to nearby cells in the epidermis (epidermal cells). The granules first are shipped to tips of long, slender projections, which branch out from the melanocyte like tentacles on an octopus (A).

The epidermal cells then "bite off" the tips of these projections (B). Once inside the epidermal cells, the precious melanosomes are moved and arranged into dark "caps," or umbrellas, over the cell's nucleus (C). These caps protect the nuclei from harmful ultraviolet light, especially when the cells divide.

UV radiation is most damaging when the epidermal cells are dividing to produce new cells. At this critical time, UV can damage the DNA (genetic information) in the nucleus, resulting in mutations and skin cancer.

The only cells that face this danger are the stem cells, the only cells in the epidermis capable of dividing. These cells reside in the deepest layer of the epidermis. And amazingly, only these vulnerable stem cells get the precious melanosomes.

There are no "white" people

Human skin is normally never truly white, though some people have less melanin in their skin than others. Surprisingly, all humans, regardless of the shade ("color") of their skin, have approximately the same number of melanocytes per square inch of skin.

Even albinos have melanocytes, but they produce colorless, rather than pigmented, melanosomes. The granules are colorless because the enzyme necessary for producing melanin is either missing or defective.

Interestingly, these colorless melanosomes are still taken into the epidermal stem cells, where they form an umbrella just as in normal skin. The result, however, is something like a clear plastic umbrella—not very good for warding off the sun.

Some people have darker skin than others, not because they have more melanocytes but because they retain a greater amount of melanin after the cells are no longer able to divide. People with lighter shades of skin break down most of their melanosomes.

While DNA is less vulnerable to UV when the cells no longer divide, retaining more pigment is still advantageous. People with darker skin are more resistant to sunburns and skin cancer. Yet people with very dark skin face another problem—they may not be able to produce enough vitamin D.

Like the miraculous plant that God provided to shade Jonah, each umbrella in our skin is a miracle for which we "have not labored, nor made it grow" (Jonah 4:10). We are no more deserving of this merciful, God-given shade than Jonah was.

Let us then give thanks for all the undeserved provisions that God has given us through Christ, who protects and sustains both our body and soul from all that might harm us. Truly, "He is not far from each one of us; for in Him we live and move and have our being" (Acts 17:27–28).

The Amazing Human Hair

by David N. Menton

Hair is mentioned over 100 times in the Bible, often in the context of God's loving care and protection for His people. For example, when God delivered Shadrach, Meshach, and Abednego from the fiery furnace, "the hair of their head was not singed" (Daniel 3:27, KJV). In Luke 21:18, Jesus warned His disciples of persecution but told them not to fear because "not a hair of your head shall be lost." Finally, Jesus declared that even "the very hairs of your head are all numbered" (Matthew 10:30, KJV). How personally and intimately our Savior knows and loves us!

Lots of hairs

The human head has an estimated 100,000 hairs, though the number varies from individual to individual. While hair appears to be largely confined to our head and a few other scattered locations, it is actually rather uniformly distributed over all our skin (with the exception of our palms and soles, which are truly hairless). On the entire surface of the human body, there are about 5 million hairs; but many of them are difficult to see.

Types of hairs

While some areas of our skin appear to lack hair (e.g., on the forehead and nose), they actually have tiny, colorless hairs called vellus hairs. We have about as many hairs per square inch on our nose and forehead as we do on the top of our head—we just don't notice them.

The long and often pigmented hairs (e.g., those of our scalp or beard) are called terminal hairs.

Several other types of hair, such as eyelashes, form during the course of our life.

The first hair follicles begin to form by the third month in the womb. The follicles produce lanugo hair. These rather long, silky hairs are usually shed in the womb a few weeks prior to birth and are replaced with vellus hairs, which grow out of the same hair follicles. A premature baby may appear surprisingly hairy because of unshed lanugo hair.

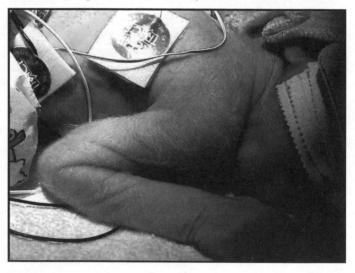

You never lose a hair follicle

Amazingly, we are born with all the hair follicles we are ever going to have, and these follicles normally continue to produce hairs throughout our lives.

Why then do so many of us get bald with age? Beginning at puberty, some follicles that had been producing terminal hairs begin to replace them with almost invisible vellus hairs. So you don't lose hairs as you age, your hair just gets smaller.

Why don't animals need a barber?

While many of us make periodic trips to the barber, most nonhuman mammals always appear in perfect trim without a barber. The reason for this is that hair grows in a cyclic manner. A relatively long period of growth (that varies with the type and location of the hair) is followed by a short period of rest after which the hair is released from the follicle, and a new growth cycle begins forming a new hair. Thus the length of the growth cycle determines the length of the hair.

If hair grew longer and longer without being released from the follicle, it would be disastrous for the mammals that don't visit a barber. Can you imagine, for example, a squirrel dashing through the branches, dragging a couple feet of hair? The Lord thinks of everything!

Hair grows about .3 mm per day (about three tenths the thickness of a dime). Within a year, our scalp and beard can produce nearly five inches (13 cm). By comparison, the longest hairs on our arm have a growth cycle of less than two months.

The growth cycle of scalp and beard hairs varies from individual to individual but can be several years. A Vietnamese man was reported to have the longest scalp hair, which measured over 20 ft. (6 m) long. According to a BBC News report in June 2004, he claimed not to have cut his hair in more than 30 years.

The growth of the human hair

Hair grows from tube-like depressions in the skin called hair follicles. The hair shaft is formed from living cells deep in the follicle. These fragile living cells subsequently die to form the remarkably strong fiber we call a hair. The same follicle is capable of producing more than one type of hair during the course of our lives.

Figure 1—Growth cycle

Growth
Hair grows from the bottom of the follicle at a rate of 3 tenths the thickness of a dime per day.

Resting
Hair grows to a certain length specific to each follicle then stops growing for a short period of time.

New growth
When growth begins again in the hair follicle, the resting hair is released from the follicle and a new hair is produced.

The hair cuticle

All hairs are covered with a layer of flattened dead cells (called the cuticle) that help to keep the hair from knotting up (imagine the knotted mess if our hair was made from comparably thin nylon thread). Under the microscope the cuticle looks like overlapping shingles or roof tiles.

Wigs made from natural human hair must have all their hairs facing in the proper direction (the free edges of the cuticle cells facing away from the scalp), if they are to be groomed and lie properly.

The shape of the cuticle has an added benefit—perhaps its most important function—it locks the hair in its follicle.

Figure 2—Structure
Magnified view of a human hair showing both mid-shaft and tip. The hair is covered with a layer of overlapping shingle-like cells called the cuticle.

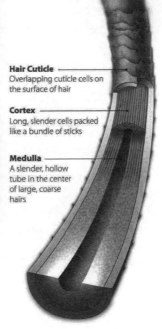

Hair Cuticle
Overlapping cuticle cells on the surface of hair

Cortex
Long, slender cells packed like a bundle of sticks

Medulla
A slender, hollow tube in the center of large, coarse hairs

The incredible "hair lock"

The hair needs to be locked inside the hair follicle to prevent it from being easily pulled out. Without a "hair lock," hair loss would likely prove fatal for most mammals.

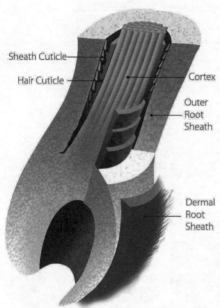

Figure 3—The incredible "hair lock"

The hair follicle is lined with a cuticle whose overlapping cells face the opposite direction of the cuticle on the hair shaft. The precise interlock of the two cuticles makes it impossible to pull out a hair without tearing out a large part of the follicle with it. But don't worry; this event immediately triggers the rebuilding of the damaged follicle and a new hair growth cycle.

The question arises, if the hair is locked in place, how does it slide out as it grows? Amazingly, tens of thousands of little "buttons," called desmosomes, line the hair follicle. These buttons are quickly buttoned and unbuttoned in a precise sequence to allow the hair to slide out in a controlled fashion. Before the hair emerges from the surface of the skin, the lock (the cuticle lining the hair follicle) is digested with special enzymes.

Figure 4—The cuticle
Cuticle cells, lining the innermost layer of the hair follicle, interlock with the cuticle on the hair shaft. On the left is a magnified view of the follicle cuticle in contact with the hair cuticle. To the right is a magnified view of the follicle cuticle peeled away from the hair showing a perfect match.

Standing in awe of hair

We stand in awe of Christ our Creator, who has lavished such exquisite design and complexity on even the hairs of our body. We are greatly comforted by Christ our Protector, who has numbered the very hairs of our head and will not permit one hair to be harmed if it is not His will. And finally, we are eternally grateful for the amazing grace of Christ our Savior who allowed His own hairs to be plucked from His cheeks as He endured taunting, torment, and death for our sins.

"I gave my back to the smiters, and my cheeks to them that plucked off the hair: I hid not my face from shame and spitting" (Isaiah 50:6, KJV).

Our Index Finger— Pointing to the Creator

by Jonathan W. Jones

Some have suggested that the elegant designs in nature are merely illusions, fortunate outcomes of natural selection. If so, we would expect to find a confusion of haphazard, incomplete, and flawed structures. But when we look more closely at something as outwardly simple as extending a finger to type the letter *u*, we discover an astoundingly sophisticated design that points unmistakably to the Creator.

Seven faithful muscles

Seven muscles are required to control the index finger (Figure 1). Let's contemplate each one briefly. The lumbrical muscle is a good place to start. Unlike most other muscles, which attach to bone, the lumbrical connects a tendon near the front of the index finger to a phenomenally complex shroud of delicate tendons and related tissues.

The lumbrical muscle serves two main functions—extending and retracting the finger in coordination with the other muscles.

These muscles must work closely together. The complexity of moving three finger bones in sync is hard to grasp. Imagine laying three steel bars on the ground end-to-end, and then tying the bars together with a series of wire harnesses. Pulling any one wire will affect the other wires. Now try moving all three bars together, side-to-side and up-and-down at the same time. You'll quickly see how hard it is to keep everything in alignment.

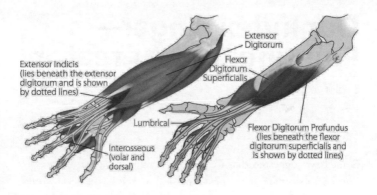

Figure 1—Seven servants of finger motion

The index finger needs seven muscles to control its movement in all directions. Four are anchored in the forearm and three in the palm. The lumbrical muscle is interesting because it doesn't attach to bones but connects muscles and tendons in a complex "net" that shifts position in response to ever-changing forces.

Yet our index finger has no such problem. As the lumbrical muscle contracts, it reduces the tension on the long flexor tendon, while the lumbrical muscle simultaneously pulls on a ligament at the side of the finger, extending the finger (Figure 2). Sound complicated? That's just a small part of the picture.

Several other muscles and tendons help control the positions of the finger bones. Consider the two long extensor muscle-tendon units. They split into three separate tendons over the first bone of the finger (Figure 3). The side tendons then shift above or below the second joint of the finger, depending on the degree to which the finger must be curled (or "flexed").

Yet these tendons cannot straighten the finger by themselves. They need the simultaneous action of four other muscles: two interosseus muscles, located in the palm of your hand, and the long flexor muscle-tendon units located in the forearm. Without all these muscles working together, the finger bones would quickly become malpositioned and nonfunctional.

Figure 2—Multi-tasking muscle tendons

By an ingenious design, the long extensor tendon performs two opposite tasks. To extend the finger, the lateral band of the tendon shifts above the joint's center rotation point and pulls the finger up, like the reins on a horse. To curl the finger, the lateral band of the tendon shifts under the center rotation point and pulls down.

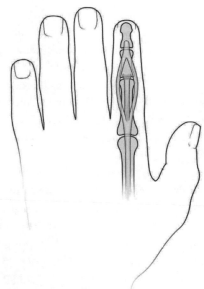

Figure 3—Three in one

To ensure complete control of your index finger, the muscles are attached in a complex configuration. For example, the long extensor tendon splits into three bands over the second knuckle. The side tendons can shift above or below the joint, depending on the finger's position.

A "wonderfully integrated"[1] relationship between muscles is required to bring about this desired motion.

Other finger motions require a different symphony of muscle movements. For instance, try shifting your finger sideways and forward, as though you are typing the letter *y*. The muscles interact in very different ways than when you type *a u*, but the motion can be just as smooth.[2,3]

The number of potential finger positions is virtually unlimited. If each of the seven muscles is capable of assuming one hundred different positions (and this is a conservative estimate) then the possible combinations would be 1x1014 or about 100 trillion. Yet our index finger can attain all of these positions with ease.

Keeping it all straight

The finger's tendons and ligaments have rightly been described as a complex, dynamic "net" that constantly shifts position in response to the multiple forces acting upon it. Can you imagine how complicated it must be to keep all these factors in balance?

Yet studies demonstrate that humans can exert such specific control of their muscles that they can direct a single nerve cell in the spinal cord to activate the few muscle fibers that the nerve cell controls.[4] Additional nerve cells can be activated if a person wants to move an entire finger joint or alter tension in one muscle. This precise control enables microsurgeons to manipulate delicate instruments to repair arteries as small as one third of a millimeter in diameter.

Shifting the index finger from one computer key to another requires little conscious effort, but such activity demands simultaneous processing of hundreds of thousands of electrical signals. Nerve cells within the spinal cord receive signals from sensors in the hand that detect motion, stretch, and position. This information, together with visual input from the eyes, enables the nervous system to make instant calculations about the finger's current position in space and immediately send new commands to multiple muscles to alter the finger's position.

Digital signal processing did not originate with computers. It has been a part of our makeup since God created the first man, Adam. The monitoring system in our spinal cord and brain stem far surpasses anything humans have yet devised. The most advanced robotics research centers have endeavored to mathematically model finger motions in just two dimensions, with only limited success.[5,6]

By elaborate biochemical processes, sensors in the hand fire volleys of on-off signals to update the central nervous system about the hand's status. If local anesthetics block these updates, then the patient will continue to perceive that the hand remains in the same position even if it moved. The central nervous system must continually reappraise incoming data to determine the positions of all voluntary parts.

This control system, which rapidly assesses incoming data from thousands of sources and then directs selected motors to respond, is apparently encoded in our DNA before birth. This "software" enables us not only to process a continuous stream of data but also to write new software subroutines that help us remember new finger motions as we practice them, whether learning to type or to play a musical instrument.

We even have special pre-installed programs to help us in emergencies. The withdrawal of a limb in response to contact with hot or sharp objects, for example, reveals this involuntary, unlearned programming, which smoothly and rapidly coordinates the action of multiple muscle groups. The physiologic process by which this "software" is written and the code is stored is not understood at all.

Effective functioning of the index finger requires not only well-orchestrated muscles, tendons, and nerves but also efficient processes to regulate blood flow, temperature, wound repair, growth, and immunity to diseases. The list goes on and on.

The question of origin

Every part of our body, including our fingers, has a clear, integrated purpose. Detailed studies of hand anatomy have failed to identify a single structure devoid of function. Those who dismiss finger motion as simply the end result of a series of accidents have failed to appreciate the complex physiology involved.

Richard Smith, a noted hand surgery educator, once postulated that the first muscles to move fingers evolved within the hand proper. He stated that the forearm muscles appeared much later.[7] Strangely, he did not acknowledge the fact that both groups of muscles must work together for effective hand function to occur.

Smith referenced the evolutionist Napier's 1965 address to the Royal Society in London[8] as evidence for the hand's evolution and further speculated that the muscles within our hands are derived from the pectoral muscles of fish. This suggestion is implausible because recent studies have revealed that the amino acid sequences of structural proteins differ significantly among species.[9]

Napier's address presented pictures of monkey and human hands and an unproved history of descent. His presentation, often quoted as authoritative, provides no evidence whatsoever of the evolution of the hand. Instead, it shows how a prior belief system drives our interpretation of the facts, even when they do not fit well.

When you look more closely under the surface of living things, one thing you don't find is a mess. Those who deny the Creator expect to find disorder and invent levels of disarray and chaos that simply do not exist. Hand surgeons see that the finger extensor mechanism is intimidatingly complex and difficult to understand. Our best efforts in reconstructing a robotic hand pale in comparison to the structure and function of the original design.

Even the simple act of moving your finger from u to y on the computer keyboard reinforces the fact that we are fearfully and wonderfully made.

1. C. Harris and G. Rutledge, "The Functional Anatomy of the Extensor Mechanism of the Finger," *J. Bone Joint Surg.* 54A, no. 4 (1972): 713.

2. S. Sunderland, "The Actions of the Extensor Digitorum Communis, Interosseus and Lumbrical Muscles," *Am. J. Anat.* 77 (1945): 189.

3. R. Chase, "Muscle Tendon Kinetics," *Am. J. Surg.* 109 (1965): 277.

4. J. V. Basmajian, "Control and Training of Individual Motor Units, *Science* 141 (1963): 440.

5. E. L. Secco and G. Magenes, "Bio-Metric Finger: Human like Morphology, Control and Motion Planning for Intelligent Robot Prosthesis," *Mobile Robots, Moving Intelligence* 325 (2006).

6. F. J. Valero-Cuevas, "An Integrative Approach to the Biomechanical Function and Neuromuscular Control of the Fingers," *J. Biomechanics* 38, no. 4 (2005): 673.

7. R. J. Smith, *Tendon Transfers of the Hand and Forearm* (Little Brown, 1987), p. 103.

8. J. R. Napier, "The Evolution of the Human Hand," *Proc. R. Soc. Lond.* 40 (1968): 544.

9. Y. K. Lin and D. C. Liv, "Comparison of Physical-Chemical Properties of Type 1 Collagen from Different Species," *Food Chemistry* 99 (2006): 244.

Dr. Jonathan Jones holds an MD from the University of California at San Diego. He completed his postgraduate training in plastic surgery at the University of Texas Medical Branch in Glaveston, Texas, and is in practice in San Diego where he does reconstructive surgery, microsurgery, and hand surgery.

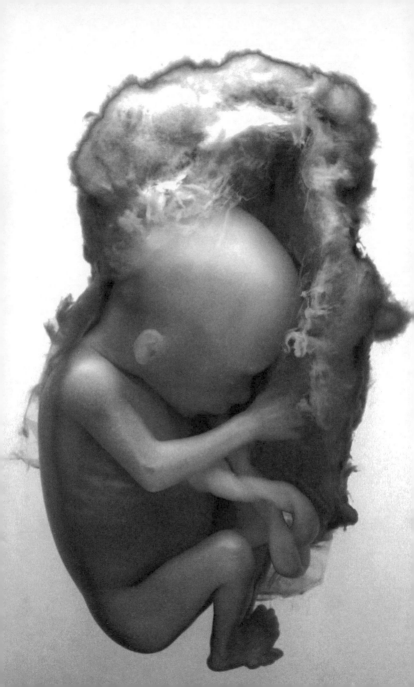

The Placenta—A Selfless Servant

by David N. Menton

*I*n the Apostle Paul's letter to the Romans, he compares the Church to the human body (Romans 12:4–8). The Church is one body made of many members, each having his own God-given gift. Likewise, we humans have one body made up of many organs, with each serving its own God-given function.

An unappreciated organ

Of all the body's organs, perhaps the one that best exemplifies selfless service is the placenta. Most people give little thought to the placenta, and few appreciate the marvelous complexity and profound importance of this organ that is discarded and forgotten after birth. While parents and loved ones lift joyful prayers of thanks for the safe arrival of their newborn, few think of thanking God for the essential services rendered by His marvelously designed creation—the placenta.

After the egg is fertilized, the placenta is the very first organ to develop. Recent studies show that when the fertilized egg divides to form the first two cells, one is already destined to form the placenta, while the other becomes the baby.

An important hormone-producing gland

As soon as three days after fertilization—weeks before the mother normally suspects she is pregnant—cells of the developing placenta, called trophoblasts, begin to produce hormones. These hormones ensure that the lining of the uterus—the endometrium—will be ready to receive the embryo's implantation. Over the next few weeks, the developing placenta begins to make hormones that control the mother's physiology in a way that ensures the proper supply of nutrients and oxygen, which are essential to the baby's growth.

By about five days after fertilization the trophoblast cells, surrounding the developing embryo, begin to fuse together to form one giant cell with many nuclei (see Figure 1). This cell is called the syncytial trophoblast. One of the first functions of this placental giant cell is to invade the uterine wall of the mother in an amazing process called implantation (see Figure 2).

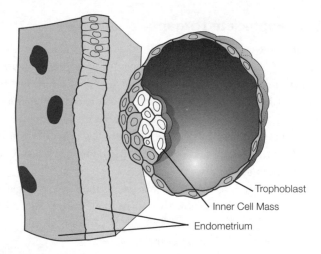

Trophoblast
Inner Cell Mass
Endometrium

Figure 1
Cross-section through the blastocyst and uterine wall about five days after fertilization. The blastocyst is a hollow fluid-filled ball, and the amazing inner cell mass is the developing baby. The cells making up the wall of the ball are trophoblast cells that will form the placenta. The endometrium of the mother's uterus is ready to receive the developing baby and its developing placenta.

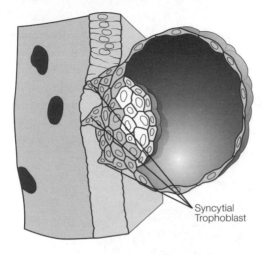

Figure 2

Cross-section through the blastocyst implanting into the uterine wall about six days after fertilization. At this time, trophoblast cells are progressively fusing together to form the syncytial trophoblast, which consists of a single giant cell with many nuclei.

Syncytial Trophoblast

Prevents the rejection of the baby as a foreign graft

Although the developing placenta and baby implant within the thick nutrient-filled wall of the mother's uterus, they are not actually part of the mother's body. One of the placenta's important roles is to protect the developing baby from an attack by the mother's immune system, since the baby and the placenta are genetically unique and distinctly different from the mother.

It is still a mystery how the placenta prevents the mother from rejecting it and the baby as a foreign graft without shutting down her immune system.

After implantation, the placental giant cell "invades" the walls of several uterine arteries and veins, causing the mother's blood to flow through channels within the cell (see Figure 3). When the baby develops its own blood and blood vessels, the mother's blood and the blood of the developing baby come into close association, but they never mix or come into direct contact. The syncytial trophoblast forms a thin, seamless, and selective barrier between maternal blood and fetal blood. All the critically important nutrients, gases, hormones, electrolytes, and antibodies that pass from mother's blood to the baby's blood must travel across this seamless and selective filter. Waste products in the baby's blood must, in turn, pass across this filter to the mother's blood.

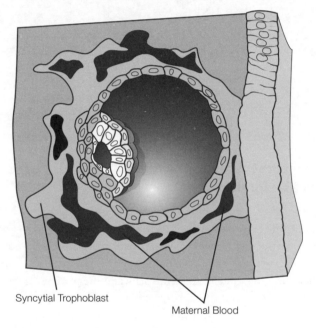

Syncytial Trophoblast

Maternal Blood

Figure 3
Cross-section of the blastocyst and endometrium about 12 days after fertilization. Maternal blood is flowing into communicating spaces that develop within the giant syncytial trophoblast cell that covers the surface of the developing placenta. The baby's blood and blood vessels have not yet developed. The baby (embryo) has now developed into two layers.

The placenta does it all!

In order to appreciate the marvelous work of the placenta, consider this: while the unborn baby's vital organs are developing and maturing, they (with the exception of the heart) are essentially useless. The placenta serves the functions of these organs by working in association with the mother. With the help of the mother's blood, the placenta must function as the baby's lungs, kidneys, digestive system, liver, and immune system. The placenta does this so well that a baby can actually survive until birth even when one or more of these vital organs sadly fail to develop in its own body.

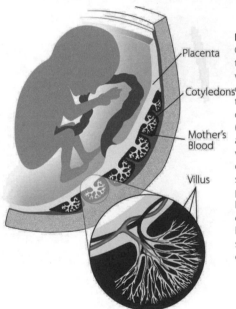

Figure 4
Cross-section through a third-trimester placenta with baby. The placenta consists of about 20 tree-like structures called cotyledons (see circular magnified area). The baby's blood vessels, arriving by way of the umbilical cord, spread out within the placenta, sending a large branch into each cotyledon. Mother's blood intimately surrounds the cotyledons

Placenta

Cotyledons

Mother's Blood

Villus

During the latter part of pregnancy, the flow of maternal blood through the placenta reaches a rate of about one pint (.5 liter) per minute. To allow an adequate surface area for exchange between mother's blood and baby's blood, the interface between the two is folded and amplified in a complex way that resembles the trunks, branches, and twigs of trees (see Figure 4). There are typically about 20 of these tree-like structures (called cotyledons) in the mature placenta. The baby's blood flows in vessels inside these cotyledons, whereas the mother's blood flows all around the outside, like air blowing through a small grove of trees. The entire surface of all the tree-like cotyledons is covered by syncytial trophoblast, forming a seamless covering, which comprises a single cell with millions of nuclei (see Figure 5). This means that the entire surface of the placenta is covered by one giant cell, which has a surface area of over 100 square feet (9.3 square meters).

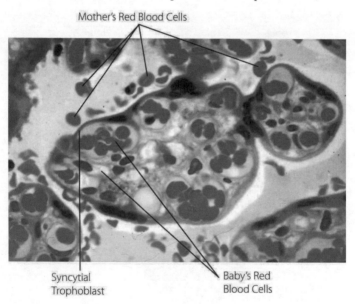

Mother's Red Blood Cells

Syncytial Trophoblast

Baby's Red Blood Cells

Figure 5

A microscope photograph of a cross-section of one of the smallest branches of a tree-like placental cotyledon at term. Mother's red blood cells surround the villus, while the baby's red blood cells are inside large capillaries within the villus. The blood of the mother and the blood of the baby are everywhere separated by the syncytial trophoblast, which is a seamless layer comprising a single cell. David Menton

The risky expulsion of the placenta after birth

During the baby's development, the placenta is securely attached to the endometrium of the uterus by some of the larger branches of each cotyledon. When the uterus contracts to expel the placenta after the birth of the baby, some of the endometrial surface is torn off with it. This results in severing about 20 large uterine arteries which, if unchecked, would involve the loss of blood at a rate of about one pint per minute. Since fewer than five quarts (4 liters) of blood are in the adult female body, all the blood would be lost in less than 10 minutes. It is also important to note that the blood-clotting mechanism is suppressed in the placenta and uterine blood vessels during pregnancy, creating a situation comparable to a hemophiliac with 20 severed arteries. These factors result in a wound that no one would expect to survive!

Saved by a miracle!

How does a woman survive childbirth with such a wound? Here is another example of the awe-inspiring work of God, the Creator and Sustainer of life. You see, each of the severed uterine arteries has a precisely placed muscular sphincter that acts like a purse string, or a surgeon's hemostat, to immediately close off the loss of blood. As a result, a normal birth involves the loss of only about a pint of blood. Simply amazing!

The next time you experience the joy of a baby's birth, thank the Lord for providing this selfless placenta. And above all, reflect on the fact that our Creator, who at the time of childbirth so mercifully spares the mother from a fatal loss of blood, did not hesitate to shed His own blood in death to save us from sin, death, and the power of the devil.

1. William J. Larson, *Human Embryology*, 2nd ed. (Saunders, 1997), pp. 33–47, 471–488.

2. Keith L. Moore, *The Developing Human: Clinically Oriented Embryology*, 4th ed. (Saunders, 1988), pp. 104–130.

3. Thomas Sadler, *Langman's Medical Embryology*, 9th ed. (Lippincott Williams & Wilkins, 2003), pp. 31–49, 51–63, 65–86.

4. Keith L. Moore and T.V.N. Persaud, *Before We Are Born*, 5th ed. (Saunders, 1998), pp. 241–254.

5. Luiz Junqueira, Jose Carneiro, and Robert Kelley, *Basic Histology*, 9th ed. (McGraw-Hill, 1998), pp. 421–445.